HowExpert Presents

How To Play Bass Guitar

Your Step By Step Guide To Playing Bass Guitar

HowExpert

For more tips related to this topic, visit HowExpert.com/bassguitar.

D1628754

Recommended Resources

- HowExpert.com – Quick 'How To' Guides on All Topics from A to Z by Everyday Experts.
- HowExpert.com/free – Free HowExpert Email Newsletter.
- HowExpert.com/books – HowExpert Books
- HowExpert.com/courses – HowExpert Courses
- HowExpert.com/clothing – HowExpert Clothing
- HowExpert.com/membership – HowExpert Membership Site
- HowExpert.com/affiliates – HowExpert Affiliate Program
- HowExpert.com/writers – Write About Your #1 Passion/Knowledge/Expertise & Become a HowExpert Author.
- HowExpert.com/resources – Additional HowExpert Recommended Resources
- YouTube.com/HowExpert – Subscribe to HowExpert YouTube.
- Instagram.com/HowExpert – Follow HowExpert on Instagram.
- Facebook.com/HowExpert – Follow HowExpert on Facebook.

Publisher's Foreword

Dear HowExpert reader,

HowExpert publishes quick 'how to' guides on all topics from A to Z by everyday experts.

At HowExpert, our mission is to discover, empower, and maximize talents of everyday people to ultimately make a positive impact in the world for all topics from A to Z...one everyday expert at a time!

All of our HowExpert guides are written by everyday people just like you and me who have a passion, knowledge, and expertise for a specific topic.

We take great pride in selecting everyday experts who have a passion, great writing skills, and knowledge about a topic that they love to be able to teach you about the topic you are also passionate about and eager to learn about.

We hope you get a lot of value from our HowExpert guides and it can make a positive impact in your life in some kind of way. All of our readers including you altogether help us continue living our mission of making a positive impact in the world for all spheres of influences from A to Z.

If you enjoyed one of our HowExpert guides, then please take a moment to send us your feedback from wherever you got this book.

Thank you and we wish you all the best in all aspects of life.

Sincerely,

BJ Min
Founder & Publisher of HowExpert
HowExpert.com

PS...If you are also interested in becoming a HowExpert author, then please visit our website at HowExpert.com/writers. Thank you & again, all the best!

Table of Contents

I.   Introduction

Where the Bass Came From

The Double bass (also known as contrabass, bass fiddle or upright bass) is the largest and lowest-pitched bowed string instrument. Its height reaches up to about 6 feet and it has four strings. The double bass can be played with a bow or by just plucking the strings.

Also called the bass violin, it is from the string family of instruments (viol family or Viola da gamba) which originated from Europe in the 15th century. The double bass was widely used during the Renaissance and Baroque periods and is still being used in Eastern European folk music.

The Electric Bass

The modern electric bass was derived from the double bass or the bass violin. Its appearance is similar to that of a guitar, but the difference is that the bass guitar has a longer neck and scale length, and has four thick strings. The bass guitar is also notated in the F clef or bass clef.

The first electric bass was invented by a musician named Paul Tutmarc in 1930. Tutmarc's bass fiddle (model 736) or bass violin has four strings with frets. The size is about 30 ½ inch scale, making the instrument easier to hold and transport.

Leo Fender created the Precision bass (P bass) in 1951. It became the first widely popular, mass-produced bass, also considered to be the first real electric bass. The Gibson Corporation then followed Fender's lead, releasing a violin shaped bass called EB-1 Bass in 1953.

Since the 1950's, Leo Fender's Precision bass (P bass) has largely replaced the double bass as the instrument of choice for making low pitched bass lines in different genres of music, although it is also used for soloing and creating melodies in jazz and funk.

What You Will Learn

In this eBook, we will concentrate specifically on how to play the electric bass. Learning the electric bass is easier than the upright bass for the following reasons:

- Formal lessons and training are not necessary to learn simple songs.
- It is used more often in most forms of music.
- It is much more convenient and portable.

Playing Bass in Rock

The electric bass, used in a rock context, can provide a good starting point for beginner bassists. Rock bass lines, compared to their classical, jazz or funk counterparts, are rarely more complicated, are more easily recognizable and can have good steady rhythms and simple, easy to follow melodies.

A novice player will also be able to play through a whole song by using a pick, rather than the fingers, which can be more difficult for beginners.

Your Role in a Band

The electric bass is typically used to play music performed by a band. Generally, your role as the bassist in the band is to provide the following:

- Support the song's beat with the drummer.
- Provide rhythm.
- Add the groove.
- Keep the steady rhythm.
- Create catchy bass lines to add textural variations to the melody of the music.

II. Lessons - Basic and Essential Knowledge for Playing

Parts of the Electric Bass

1. **Body - This is the largest part of the bass guitar.**

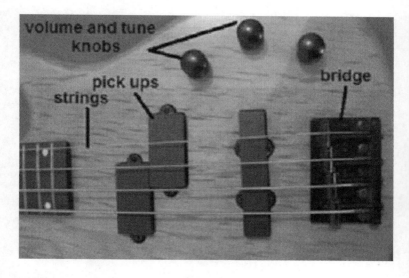

In the body, you will find the following:

- **Bridge -** This is where the strings are attached.
- **Pickups -** The magnetic pickups convert the vibrations of the strings to an electrical signal that can be recorded or amplified.

- **Volume and Tune Controls/Knobs -** You can control the overall loudness of the pickups by using the volume knob, while the tone knob is used to switch between a brighter and a more muffled sound quality.
- **Strap pins -** This is where the strap is attached.
- **Jack socket -** This is where the cable or cord is plugged in.#

2. Neck

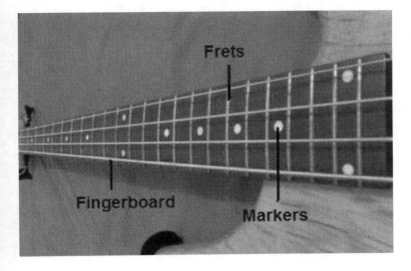

- **Fingerboard -** This is the flat side of the neck that contains the frets.
- **Frets -** These are the lines or the strips of metal embedded along the fingerboard.

3. Head/Headstock

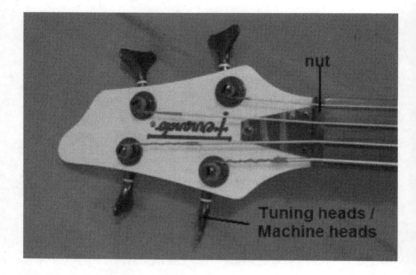

- **Nut -** This is where the strings lie at the end of the neck. The nut helps hold the strings in place.
- **Tuning Heads or Machine Heads -** Holds the end of the strings. This is where you can increase or decrease the pitch of the strings.

How to Tune the Bass Guitar

Tuning the bass can be challenging for most beginners since their ears may not yet be able to recognize specific pitches.

The best way to tune your bass correctly is to use an electronic tuner. An electronic tuner is a worthwhile investment and is the preferred way of tuning the bass since it is more accurate than tuning by ear.

How to Hold the Bass Guitar

How to Play Bass Guitar Sitting Down

Sitting is usually the best position for beginner players. You will be able to play in a more relaxed position, since your arms, back and hands won't tense up from the weight of the bass.

1. Use a stool or a chair without armrests.
2. You can play without the strap, but it is usually much more comfortable to play with it.
3. Rest your bass on your right thigh.

How to Play Bass Guitar Standing Up

Playing in the standing position can be more difficult, but it will become easier once fretting and picking become more familiar and unconscious.

1. Make sure that your strap is attached securely to the strap pins. Adjust the strap so that the body of the bass hangs around your stomach area, with the neck pointing approximately 45 degrees upward.

2. This seems to be the ideal playing position for most players, although you can adjust the bass to a position that you are comfortable with.
3. Let the bass hang freely from your shoulder.

Left Hand Tips

Fretting Tips

You will use your four fingers for fretting (numbered from 1 to 4), from your index finger (1st) to your pinky finger (4th).

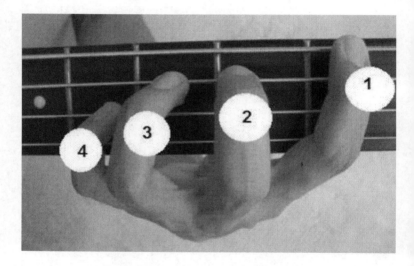

Rest your thumb lightly on the back of the neck, pointing it upward. This will help your fingers correctly fret the strings.

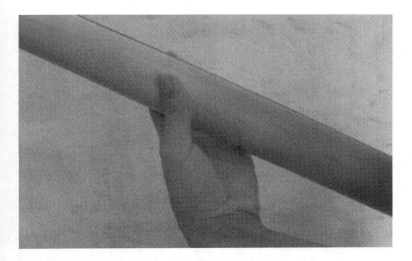

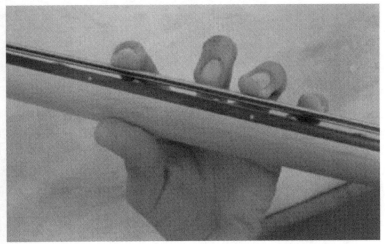

The wrist should not be overly bent. Some degree of bending is okay, as long as it does not cause the arm, wrist or hand to tense.

Right Hand Tips

Picking with a Plectrum

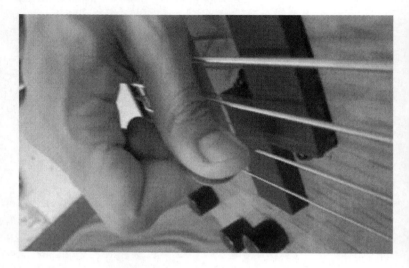

You need to find the right type of pick. Use heavy and medium gauge picks for bass. Thin picks are usually used for guitar.

1. Hold the pick between the thumb and the first finger (index finger) of the right (picking) hand.
2. Use the tip of the pick (the pointed end) for picking.
3. The most basic picking strokes you will need to learn are the down stroke, when you push the tip of the pick down against the string, and an upstroke, when you pull the tip of the pick upward to pluck the string. Finally, alternate picking is the combination of down strokes and upstrokes.

Finger Style Picking Tips

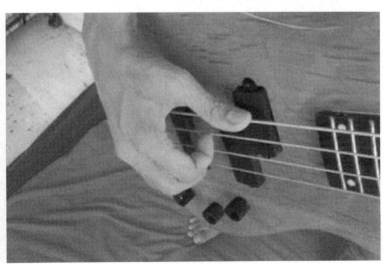

1. Keep your plucking hand, wrist and arm relaxed.
2. There are two positions you can use when using finger-style picking. Some players like to rest their thumb on a pickup while others rest their forearms on the bass body and let their right-hand hang freely, resting the thumb ever-so-slightly on the 4th string (E). The first method uses the thumb as the fulcrum to put power into your plucking, while the second uses wrist movement to put power into your plucking.
3. While you can use all of your fingers to pluck the strings, it is recommended that beginners use only the 1st finger (index finger) and your 2nd finger (middle finger) for plucking. Use them alternately.
4. Let your fingers roll over the top of your strings.

How To Play Reading Notation

We will start with only the basic symbols and terminologies necessary for you to be able to read the musical notation of popular songs. Some songs have a lot more symbols, but those are more suitable for intermediate to advanced players.

Once you have mastered the basics, you can move on to the next level to learn more symbols and terminologies.

Basic Musical Symbols and Notations

The Staff

The staff is made up of five horizontal lines with four spaces. This is where musical symbols are written. The lines and spaces correspond to letters of the musical alphabet (A, B, C, D, E, F, G)

The Clef

The clef is a musical symbol written at the beginning of the staff. This will help you identify the pitch of the notes written on the staff.

The Difference Between G clef and F clef

This is the **G-clef or the treble clef**. It is used for *higher pitched* instruments like piccolo, flute, oboe, clarinet and trumpet.

This is the **F-clef or the bass clef**. This is used for *lower pitched* notes like bass, timpani, contrabass, cello and trombone.

The treble clef always starts on letter **C**, while the bass clef always starts on letter **E**.

Since bass guitar is a low-pitched instrument, we are going to focus more on reading notes in the F-clef or the bass clef.

Sharp and Flat

♯ **The sharp sign** looks very similar to the number sign (#). You will often find this after the F-clef or beside the note. This sign means that the note is a half step higher, one fret closer to the body of the bass.

♭ **The flat symbol** looks like a small letter "b". You will often find this after the F-clef or beside the note. This sign means "lower in pitch", or that the note is a half step lower, one fret closer to the neck of the bass.

Musical Notations and Rests

In this section you will need to memorize each kind of note as well as the rest counts.

The value of a note indicates its duration, or how long it should ring out.

Rests indicate the duration of silence, or how long you should pause.

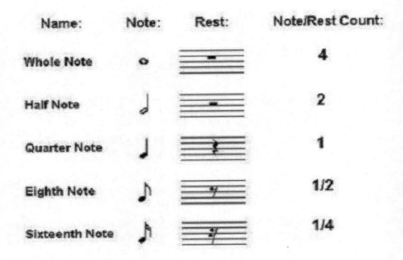

Name:	Note:	Rest:	Note/Rest Count:
Whole Note			4
Half Note			2
Quarter Note			1
Eighth Note			1/2
Sixteenth Note			1/4

How to Count

Beginners will find it easier to count notes out loud and slowly. It is also recommended that you tap your foot along to the counts, though this should be eliminated as you progress. You should count internally once it becomes natural to you.

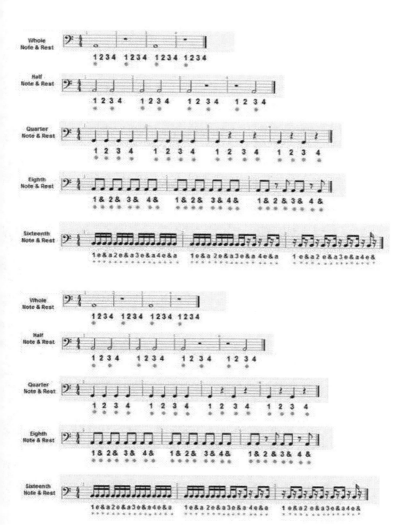

Dotted Note

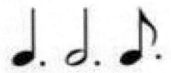

A note or a rest with a dot beside it is called a dotted note. When you see a dotted note or dotted rest, this means you will have to add a beat that is half the value of the note or rest that is dotted. For example, a half note has 2 beats. If it is a dotted half note, you need to add one more beat, which gives a dotted half note a total of 3 counts or beats.

Repeat Symbol

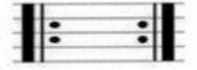

You will see this symbol at the beginning of the bar line (bar lines are the lines that divide the staff) and at the end of the staff. If you see this symbol, you will need to repeat the section from the first repeat symbol. The upper part of the end of the bar line indicates how many times you need to repeat it.

Time Signatures

Time signature will help you identify how many beats are in each measure. Time signatures are located right after the clef. The lower of the two numbers indicates the note value equivalent to one beat. The upper number indicates how many of these notes are in one measure.

Downbeat

Downbeat is the first beat in a measure. Downbeat is measured by the downward stroke of the conductor's baton at the beginning of the song/measure.

Reading Tablature Tips

What is a Tablature

Tablature (or tabs for short) is another method of writing music made for fretted instruments like guitar and bass. Tabs will tell you the exact location of the note that you are going to play. However, many online tabs will not tell you the note durations.

How to Read Tabs

1. Bass tabs will have four lines corresponding to the 4 strings of your bass. Some bass tabs will have more lines because some basses have more than 4 strings. The top line on the tab is the G string (the thinnest string) and the bottom line is the E string (the thickest string).

2. The numbers indicate the fret number; it is written on the string where it should be played. For the above example: Place your finger on the 3rd fret of the A string, then use the next finger to press the same string at the 5th fret and so on. Zero indicates an open string, which means you just need to pluck on the string without fretting anything. Finally, tabs are read from left to right.

III. Lessons – Song Demonstration

Nirvana - Smells Like Teen Spirit: Reading notation, picking using a plectrum

For teaching purposes, we will talk about two well-known songs that sound great on the bass guitar.

This first song has repeating lines that are catchy and easy to remember. It is not overly difficult, but does have a few passages that can challenge a beginner. This is a good piece to help familiarize yourself with finger positioning.

Look over the sheet music carefully before you begin. You will see a lot of dotted notes, rests and tied notes, but try not to be confused by this. As you familiarize yourself with the score, you will notice that there are repeating patterns throughout the song that will quickly become familiar.

I suggest that you use the lower position for this song, closer to the neck, instead of playing notes further up the fretboard. This can help you get a fuller sound with more sustain, and playing in a higher position can be difficult at first. If you want a tighter and heavier sound, play on the thicker strings but on a position higher up the fretboard.

You can use alternate picking just to familiarize yourself with the notes and the overall sound of the song. When you have memorized the song, you can then use down strokes for some of the passages to give them more emphasis. Using down strokes (using a plectrum/pick) will give you a more intense sound. This is recommended for this song, especially for the intro and the chorus.

Smells Like Teen Spirit
Nirvana
Nevermind
Words & Music by Dave "The Fit Bean" Clark

Suggested Playing Tips

Intro:

- The bass line begins with 4 whole rests and a dotted half rest (1,2,3,4; 1,2,3,4; 1,2,3,4) + 3. You will have to count to 15 while the guitar is playing the intro riff.
- Place your fretting hand and index finger on the 9th fret of the E string while counting down. This is the first note you will play.
- Then move your hands to the first fret (near the head). Use your index finger to play the notes on the first fret.
- Look carefully: there is a dotted quarter note, as well as an inverted ark. For these tied notes, or paired notes, you will only play the first note of the pair. Play those paired notes as one.
- Next, place your pinky finger (4th) on the 4th fret of the E string. For beginners, it can be painful at first, but this is a good exercise for your fingers. Make sure that you move your hand to that position as well, and remember that your thumbs should always point upward as much as possible.
- Repeat notes from the first fret to the 4th fret.

Verse:

- From the 4th fret, move your hands or place your index finger (1st) on the first fret of the E string, then use your index finger to play the notes on the first fret.
- Then move your pinky (4th) to the 4th fret of the E string. Let your pinky finger play all of the notes on the 4th fret.
- You will repeat these steps 10 times

Chorus:

- You are going to repeat the notes played in the intro (except for the C# or the note on the 9th fret of the E string). Repeat this 6 times.
- Remember to use your index finger to play the notes on the 1st fret and your pinky finger to play the notes on the 4th fret.
- Use your index finger (1st) to play the strings on the first fret, use your middle finger (2nd) to play the notes on the 2nd fret.
- Then move your fretting hand and place it so that your pinky finger (4th) plays the notes on the 6th fret.
- Then use your middle finger (2nd) to play the notes on the 4th fret.
- For the second verse, you will just play the same notes that you used for the first verse, until you get to the chorus.
- After the chorus, play the notes used in the chorus 8 times, then play the notes used in the verse 10 times, then play the notes used in the chorus again 6 more times.

Notes used:

Intro:

F (1st fret, E string), A# (1st fret, A string), A (Open A string), G# (4th fret, E string), C# (4th fret, A string), A (Open A string).

Verse:

F (1st fret, E string), A# (1st fret, A string), G# (4th fret, E string), C# (4th fret, A string).

Chorus:

F (1st fret, E string), A# (1st fret, A string), A (Open A string), G# (4th fret, E string), C# (4th fret, A string), A (Open A string).

F (1st fret, E string), E (Open E string), F (1st fret, E string), F# (2nd fret, E string), F# (2nd fret, E string), F (1st fret, E string), E (Open E string), F (1st fret, E string), A# (1st fret, A string), G# (4th fret, E string).

The Beatles - Can't Buy Me Love: Tablature and Finger Style Picking

Now we are going to talk about the second of our example songs. We want to help you play this song because it is very popular and quite easy to play for beginners.

The bass lines of this song use quarter notes until the end, but are done in a medium, up-tempo shuffle groove. This is good practice for steady picking, while also placing a slight emphasis on some of the notes.

Before anything else, practice each note slowly and let your fingers become familiarized with the patterns.

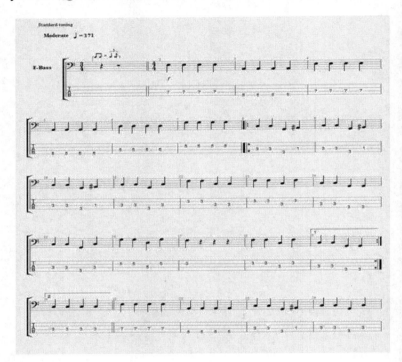

Suggested Playing Tips

Intro:

- Begin with a downbeat (3 counts before playing the first note of the song, indicated by a quarter rest and a half rest at the beginning).
- While counting, place your hand so that your fingers can reach the 7th fret of the A string and 5th fret of the E string.
- Use your ring finger (3rd) to play the note on the 7th fret.
- Use your index finger (2nd) to play the notes on the 5th fret, from the E string to D string.

Verse:

- Move your hands to the 3rd fret.
- Use your ring finger (3rd) to play the notes on the 3rd fret. You will be playing the notes on the 3rd fret of the A string, then moving your ring finger up to the E string.
- Next, use your index finger (1st) to play the note on the 1st fret of the A string.
- Then return to the 3rd fret. You will be playing a lot of notes on the 3rd fret, from the D string to the E string.
- On the 15th measure, move your hands to the 5th fret and use your ring finger (3rd) to play the notes on the 5th fret.
- The note transitions can be confusing at first. If you cannot do it at first, try playing it at a slower tempo and repeat the pattern until you get it right.
- Go over measure 17 carefully; it has one quarter note and 3 quarter rests. This means you will have to pause for three beats.

- The next note is still on the 3rd fret.
- You will need to repeat the verse two times.

Chorus:

- Use your index finger (1st) to play the notes on the 3rd fret.
- Then move your hand and use your ring finger (3rd) to play the notes on the 7th fret. You will need to use your index finger in playing the next note on the 5th fret.
- Then move your hand to the 3rd fret and let your ring finger (3rd) play the note on the 3rd fret.

Verse 2:

- Repeat verse part once.
- Then move your hand to the 3rd fret.
- Use your ring finger (3rd) to play the notes on the 3rd fret. You will be playing the notes on the 3rd fret of the A string then moving your ring finger up to the E string.
- Then, use your index finger (1st) to play the note on the 1st fret of the A string.
- Then return to the 3rd fret. You will be playing a lot of notes on the 3rd fret, from the D string to the E string.
- On the 15th measure, move your hands to the 5th fret and use your ring finger (3rd) to play the notes on the 5th fret.

- Remember there are 3 quarter rests, so do not forget to pause for 3 beats.
- The next note that you are going to play is still on the 3rd fret.
- You will repeat the verse two more times.

Solo:

- There will be additional notes here. I suggest you play it at a slower tempo to memorize it.
- On the 34th measure, use your index finger to play the notes on the 3rd fret.
- Use your ring finger play the note on the 5th fret of the A string.
- Then, use your pinky to play the note on the 6th fret, A string (D#).
- Finally, move your hand near the 2nd fret and let your index finger play the note on the 2nd fret of the D string.

Conclusion

How to Clean & Maintain Your Bass Guitar

Cleaning Tips

Wipe the body and the neck of the bass carefully with a dry cloth after playing. Flannel is a good material for cleaning, as it does not shed many fibers that can get between the instrument's hardware. Metal parts (frets, strings, pickups, tuning heads, strap pins) are especially susceptible to tarnish because of the sweat from your hands. Rub these with a bit of machine oil (WD-40) immediately after playing and leave a small amount of oil if possible. This will help maintain the hardware's shiny appearance.

Storage Tips

Instruments like basses are best stored inside a hard or soft case (see above). It should be stored somewhere dry at a comfortable temperature.

Although electric basses are relatively tougher instruments compared to acoustic guitars and other hollow body instruments, you should avoid leaving them in places that can get very hot, like the inside of a car, as this can warp the wooden parts.

Practice Tips

Correct practice habits are essential to your growth as a bassist. Simply practicing without being systematic and structured can be a waste of time. There are many things you need to do when practicing, but before anything else you will need to establish when and where you will practice.

Practice Space/Location

Here are some tips on where to practice playing your bass:

- Find a comfortable place where you will be able to play at a high volume without disturbing anyone.
- Concentration is key. Find a place where you will not be distracted by anything or anyone. Avoid turning on your computer, answering calls and the like.
- Find a place where everything you need for practicing is within your reach.

Practice Time/Regimen

A professional musician usually spends several hours in continuous practice every day. This is the best way to improve. However, if you do not have this luxury, you will need to find some way to squeeze in a bit of regular practice time.

Practicing regularly for less time often produces better results than practicing for long periods of time infrequently.

Further, learning music is very similar to working out: Just as muscles need time to rest after the gym, your fingers, hands, arms and even your mind need time to rest and "absorb" everything that you have learned during practice.

Without rest, you also run the risk of getting "burnt out", physically and mentally exhausted, including causing damage to your hands. Long practice sessions are not bad, but frequency should always take precedence over duration.

Practice Routine

As mentioned earlier, you will need to focus on different aspects of your playing every time you practice. You will need to divide your practice time among several areas of study, so you will be able to learn more efficiently and systematically. Important activities include:

- **Warm up and drills** - Spend some time at the beginning of your practice time to warm up your fingers. A good warm-up routine for beginners would be to play the major scale at different positions at the neck. Start slow to give your hand time to adjust to the movement. It is very important that you use a metronome, drum machine or anything that will help you keep the correct beat. This will help you build a strong internal tempo.
- **Sight reading** - This is often neglected by musicians who have not undergone formal training, but it is very important for your development as a player. A person who knows how to read music can perform almost anywhere or anytime, as long as he has sheet music. You must focus on training how to read notation, and not tabs. Notation is the standard for all musicians and will give you the complete information about any piece of music.
- **Ear training** - This will probably take up the majority of your practice time. A good ear-training activity would be to learn songs you like without using notation or tabs. Learning songs by ear would not only train your ear to recognize different notes and patterns, it will help you add more songs to your repertoire. Learning songs is also much better practice than working on drills, since you will be able to work on scales and arpeggios in a musical context rather than by mere repetition.
- **Jamming and Improvisation** - Jamming may come later, after you get used to playing scales across the fretboard. Improvisation

helps you learn the notes all over the fretboard and brings out your creativity as well.

Practicing these areas will help you develop into an overall well-rounded player.

Do not forget to take breaks during practices. Take a 15-minute break for an hour's practice. You may feel a bit of pain or tension building up in your fingers, wrist and arms after playing for a while. If so, simply shake your hands and arms to release tension, and do not forget to stretch your back and neck. Stretching is important, and will help you avoid pain and permanent damage in the back and arms.

Passion and Inspiration

Now that you know the basics of how to play bass, you can try playing your favorite songs or even compose your own. Further, the bass is not limited to providing grooves in the background; it is a very versatile instrument with which you can create melodies.

Many of famous players like Victor Wooten and Billy Sheehan are able to play the bass as a solo instrument. Just like with any instrument, there are limitless possibilities with the bass. However, the most important thing is for you to be able to play for your own enjoyment.

Passion for music is essential in this journey. Your instrument is your voice; it will sing for you. Practicing and training will give you the skills to express yourself better through your instrument. Mastery will take hard work and dedication, but these will not be obstacles for someone who is passionate about his craft.

Finally, inspiration is what fuels your creativity. You will need constant sources of inspiration, whether it is your life experiences or the music of others. Since playing is an expression of personal feelings, your playing will show how inspired you are, and your listeners will be sure to notice this.

Bibliography

- Naindenov, Eugeny "Ultimate Guitar", Smells Like Teen Spirit Guitar Pro Ver2
    - *http://www.ultimate-guitar.com/tabs/n/nirvana/smells_like_teen_spirit_ver2_guitar_pro.htm*
    - *(Music sheet for the song Smells like teen spirit by Nirvana)*
        - *http://www.rockmystrings.com/uploads/5/1/2/1/5121917/smells_like_teen_spirit.pdf*
        - *Dave "The Fit Bean" Clark*
- Naindenov, Eugeny "Ultimate Guitar", Can't Buy Me Love Guitar Ver2
    - *http://tabs.ultimate-guitar.com/b/beatles/cant_buy_me_love_ver2_guitar_pro.htm*
    - *(Tabs for the song Can't Buy Me Love by the Beatles)*
- *Nirvana. "Smells like Teen Spirit".*
- *The Beatles. "Can't Buy Me Love".*

Recommended Resources

- HowExpert.com – Quick 'How To' Guides on All Topics from A to Z by Everyday Experts.
- HowExpert.com/free – Free HowExpert Email Newsletter.
- HowExpert.com/books – HowExpert Books
- HowExpert.com/courses – HowExpert Courses
- HowExpert.com/clothing – HowExpert Clothing
- HowExpert.com/membership – HowExpert Membership Site
- HowExpert.com/affiliates – HowExpert Affiliate Program
- HowExpert.com/writers – Write About Your #1 Passion/Knowledge/Expertise & Become a HowExpert Author.
- HowExpert.com/resources – Additional HowExpert Recommended Resources
- YouTube.com/HowExpert – Subscribe to HowExpert YouTube.
- Instagram.com/HowExpert – Follow HowExpert on Instagram.
- Facebook.com/HowExpert – Follow HowExpert on Facebook.

Printed by Amazon Italia Logistica S.r.l.
Torrazza Piemonte (TO), Italy

49579088R00027